ADVEN

Advent with St. Francis

DAILY REFLECTIONS

Diane M. Houdek

Franciscan
MEDIA
Cincinnati, Ohio

Cover image ©The Crosiers | Gene Plaisted, o.s.c.
Cover and book design by Mark Sullivan.

LIBRARY OF CONGRESS CATALOGING-IN-PUBLICATION DATA
Houdek, Diane M.
Advent With St. Francis : Daily Reflections / Diane M. Houdek.
pages cm
ISBN 978-1-61636-705-3
1. Advent—Prayers and devotions. 2. Christmas—Prayers and devotions.
3. Catholic Church—Prayers and devotions. I. Francis, of Assisi, Saint,
1182-1226. Works. Selections. English. II. Title.
BV40.H665 2013
242'.332—dc23

2013013732

ISBN 978-1-61636-705-3

Published by Franciscan Media
28 W. Liberty St.
Cincinnati, OH 45202
www.FranciscanMedia.org

Printed in the United States of America.
Printed on acid-free paper.
13 14 15 16 17 5 4 3 2 1

Contents

Introduction
"Let Us Begin Again"

I have two favorite quotes from St. Francis. The first is "Let us begin again, for until now we have done nothing." Francis said this as he was nearing his death, knowing that conversion is never a single moment but a lifelong journey. We constantly need to renew our commitment to Christ, to following the Gospel, to drawing closer to God. Advent, the beginning of a new liturgical year, is a perfect time to begin again, a fresh start for each of us.

When I was a child, Advent was a big part of my family's seasonal celebrations. An Advent calendar and a Jesse Tree hung on the wall. The Advent wreath occupied the center of the dining room table and every evening we knelt around the table and took turns reciting the Advent novena, beginning on the Feast of

St. Andrew (November 30) and ending on Christmas Eve. My next encounter with Advent was when I was a stressed and overwhelmed graduate student. I was home early for Christmas and let myself be persuaded to go to an Advent reconciliation service that ended up changing my life. Ever since then, Advent has always been a time of darkness and quiet, the calm before the bustle of the Christmas holidays. But it is also a time of much-needed rest, even solitude, time to sort out priorities and seek healing for life's inevitable stress. Advent is a time of resting and waiting. My favorite images betray my upper Midwestern roots: early winter sunsets, deep blue tinged with lavender, fallow fields marked with a dusting of snow, bare trees etched black against the sky.

Throughout the season of Advent, we explore the mystery of the Incarnation, Jesus letting go of divine splendor to embrace a human existence. In doing so, he raised all of humanity to its divine destiny. For St. Francis, meditation on this mystery was at the heart of his understanding of God's saving love for us. It was also at the heart of Francis's wholehearted embrace of poverty, of humility, of all of the divine virtues. If Jesus could let go of so much, surely Francis could let go of his luxurious lifestyle and his quest for glory and admiration. In doing so, he showed his friends and all of his followers through the centuries how to let go of the pride and possessions that kept them from living the Gospel to its fullest extent.

Advent at the time of Francis was a penitential season, much like Lent. The austerities of the season were a reminder to let go of human vanity and embrace a more divine humility. In this spirit, we might focus our Advent activities on prayer, on charity, and on reflecting on the true meaning of Christmas. There will be plenty of time for parties after December 25, and we will come to them refreshed and renewed.

My second favorite Francis quote is, "I have done what is mine to do. May Christ show you what is yours to do." Francis knew that it was important that those who followed him never lost sight of the fact that they were ultimately following Christ. It's not about a slavish imitation of a man who lived in the Middle Ages in a small town in central Italy but about seeing through his life the message of Christ for all people in all times and places.

Pope Benedict XVI said of St. Francis: "He simply wanted to gather the People of God to listen anew to the word—without evading the seriousness of God's call by means of learned commentaries" (*Jesus of Nazareth*, p. 79). In this little book, I have tried to pair the lectionary readings with the words and deeds of Francis to show how one man lived the Gospel, so that we can no longer deny that such a life is impossible. Difficult, yes—even St. Francis would admit that. But undertaken with love and the grace of God, the journey can at least begin.

First Sunday of Advent
WAKE FROM YOUR SLEEP!

Year A: Isaiah 2:1–5; Psalm 122:1–2, 3–4, 4–5, 6–7, 8–9;
Romans 13:11–14; Matthew 24:37–44 Year B: Isaiah
63:16b–17, 19b; 64:2–7; Psalm 80:2–3, 15–16, 18–19; 1
Corinthians 1:3–9; Mark 13:33–37
Year C: Jeremiah 33:14–16; Psalm 25:4–5, 8–9, 10, 14 (1b);
1 Thessalonians 3:12—4:2; Luke 21:25–28, 34–36

St. Paul tells the Romans, "You know what time it is,
how now is the moment for you to wake from sleep.
For salvation is nearer to us now than when we became
believers." And Jesus tells his disciples, "Keep therefore
awake for you do not know on what day your Lord is
coming." They're not saying this to frighten us, but to
make sure we don't miss the wonder that is Emmanuel.
Advent is a wake-up call to the Church, a time when
we're prodded into beginning again, taking more notice
of our spiritual surroundings, once again getting going
on the work of the kingdom in the world. For some of
us, if we've neglected the spiritual side of our lives, this
wake-up call is going to jar us into awareness, and at
times we will want to pull a metaphorical pillow over

our heads and pretend that it's still dark. For others of us, it's a welcome opportunity for a fresh start.

The season of Advent calls us to wake up and be aware of the presence of God in our lives and in our world. It's a gentler wake-up call than the more rigorous season of Lent but, nonetheless, we need to respond.

During Advent we recall both the beginning of Jesus's time on this earth and his return in glory. Our readings remind us that we who have been baptized into the life and death of Jesus have nothing to fear from the end of time. This is not to say we have the luxury of waiting passively for the Second Coming, secure—even complacent—in the confidence that Jesus was born, died on the cross, and saved us, and all we have to do is wait until he comes to take us home. The promise of the Second Coming contains an insistent challenge. The Gospels show us the way to work for the fullness of the kingdom.

In the first volume of *Jesus of Nazareth*, Pope Benedict said this: "It is above all by looking at Francis of Assisi that we see clearly what the words 'Kingdom of God' mean. Francis stood totally within the Church, and at the same time it is in figures such as he that the Church grows toward the goal that lies in the future, and yet is already present: The Kingdom of God is drawing near…" (p. 79).

Prayer

Our hearts desire the warmth of your love
and our minds are searching for the light of your
Word.
Give us the strength to grow in love
that the dawn of Christ's coming
may find us rejoicing in his presence
and welcoming the light of his truth.

—Alternative Opening Prayer, First Sunday of
Advent, 1974 Sacramentary

Monday of the First Week of Advent
PEACE AND GOOD

Isaiah 2:1–5 (alternate for Year A, Isaiah 4:2–6); Psalm
122:1–2, 3–4, (4–5, 6–7) 8–9; Matthew 8:5–11

The creative power of God draws people together. We recognize that creative power stirring in our lives and respond to it. "Come, let us go up to the mountain of the LORD," the people say in the First Reading from Isaiah. They are drawn by what they see there.

From the beginning, Francis encouraged this inviting approach:

In all his preaching, before he proposed the word of God to those gathered about, he first prayed for peace for them, saying: "The Lord give you peace." He always most devoutly announced peace to men and women, to all he met and overtook. For this reason many who had hated peace and had hated also salvation embraced peace, through the cooperation of the Lord, with all their heart and were made children of peace and seekers after eternal salvation.

Francis used gentle persuasion and good example rather than bullying and condemnation to lead people to Christ. Peace is the greatest promise the Lord offers his disciples. It's the great promise of this season.

Prayer

For the sake of my relatives and friends
I will say, "Peace be within you."
For the sake of the house of the LORD our God,
I will seek your good.

—Psalm 122:8–9

Tuesday of the First Week of Advent
OVERCOMING FEAR

Isaiah 11:1–10; Psalm 72:1, 7–8, 12–13, 17; Luke 10:21–24

Today's First Reading from Isaiah is one of the iconic images of the Kingdom of God, in which all creatures live in peace with one another: "The wolf shall live with the lamb, / the leopard shall lie down with the kid /… / They will not hurt or destroy / on all my holy mountain; / for the earth will be full of the knowledge of the LORD."

St. Francis spoke again: "Brother Wolf, since you are willing to make and keep this peace pact, I promise you that I will have the people of this town give you food every day as long as you live, so that you will never again suffer from hunger, for I know that whatever evil you have been doing was done because of the urge of hunger. But, my Brother Wolf, since I am obtaining such a favor for you, I want you to promise me that you will never hurt any animal or man. Will you promise me that?"… And as St. Francis held out his hand to receive the pledge, the wolf also raised its front paw and meekly and gently put it in St. Francis's hand as a sign that it was giving its pledge…. From that day, the wolf and the people kept the pact which St. Francis made.

We love the image from Isaiah and this charming story of Francis and the wolf of Gubbio precisely because we know how difficult it is to overcome the natural fear and anger that rise up in us when we lose touch with God's spirit within us. Draw on your past experiences in seeking to resolve some conflict in your circle of friends or within your own soul.

Prayer

In his days may righteousness flourish
and peace abound, until the moon is no more.

—Psalm 72:7

Wednesday of the First Week of Advent
BE FILLED WITH GOD'S LOVE
Isaiah 25:6–10; Psalm 23:1–3, 3–4, 5, 6; Matthew 15:29–37

The Scriptures describe the fullness of God's reign as a banquet of rich food and choice wines. And the Gospels tell of Jesus feeding the five thousand a simple meal of barley loaves and fish, the essential stuff of life. The many feasts we share this season can bring us closer to one another and to God. In your feasting, be mindful of those who go hungry.

Francis's first biographer, Thomas of Celano, tells this story of Francis inviting his doctor to dinner when the brothers had nothing to eat:

> When Francis was staying in a certain hermitage near Rieti, a doctor visited him daily to take care of his eyes. But one day the saint said to the brothers: "Invite the doctor and give him something very good to eat." The guardian answered him, saying: "Father, we blush to say that we are ashamed to invite him, because we are now so poor." The saint replied, saying: "Do you want me to tell you again?" The doctor, who was standing

by, said: "Dearest brothers, I will consider your poverty a real delicacy." The brothers hurried and placed upon the table all they had in their storeroom, namely, a little bread, not much wine, and, that they might eat a bit more sumptuously, the kitchen provided some vegetables. Meanwhile the table of the Lord had compassion on the table of his servants. There was a knock at the door and it was answered quickly. Behold, a certain woman offered them a basket full of fine bread, fishes and lobster pies, honey and grapes. The table of the poor brothers rejoiced at the sight of these things, and keeping the common things for the next day, they ate the better things that day.

Prayer

You prepare a table before me
   in the presence of my enemies;
you anoint my head with oil;
   my cup overflows.

—Psalm 23:5

Thursday of the First Week of Advent
HEAD FOR HIGH GROUND
Isaiah 26:1–6; Psalm 118:1, 8–9, 19–21, 25–27a;
Matthew 7:21, 24–27

We smile at the Gospel story of the man who built his house on sand, only to have it washed away in the first heavy storm. We know better than that, surely. But when we face a crisis, do we feel as if our lives have been washed out from under us? Perhaps we need to do some work on our foundation.

At the very beginning of Francis's conversion, the Lord taught him the importance of a good foundation:

He was walking one day near the church of St. Damian, which had nearly fallen to ruin and was abandoned by everyone. Led by the Spirit, he went in and fell down before the crucifix in devout and humble supplication; and smitten by unusual visitations, he found himself other than he had been when he entered. While he was thus affected, something unheard of before happened to him: the painted image of Christ crucified moved its lips and spoke. Calling him by name it said: "Francis, go, repair my house, which, as you see, is falling completely to ruin." Trembling, Francis was not a little amazed and became almost deranged by these words. He prepared himself to obey and gave himself completely to the fulfillment of this command.

Prayer

O give thanks to the LORD, for he is good;
  his steadfast love endures for ever!

—Psalm 118:1

Friday of the First Week of Advent
OPEN YOUR EYES TO THE WONDER OF GOD
Isaiah 29:17–24; Psalm 27:1, 4, 13–14; Matthew 9:27–31

We marvel at stories of Jesus healing those who cannot see. When we hear stories of people we know who have their sight restored through cataract surgery, do we also marvel at the way God continues to work miracles in today's world?

St. Francis contracted a serious eye disease when he was traveling in the east. He willingly underwent an extreme treatment for it. Although he wasn't healed, he found peace and even joy in the process, knowing that he was in God's hands.

At the time when Francis suffered the infirmity of his eyes and was persuaded to permit treatment of them, a doctor was called to the place. When he came, he brought an iron for cauterizing and ordered it to be put into the fire until it should be red-hot. But the blessed father, strengthening his body now struck with horror, spoke thus to the fire: "My brother fire, that surpasses all other things in beauty, the Most High created you strong, beautiful, and useful. Be kind to me in this hour, be courteous. For I have loved you in the past in the Lord. I beseech the great Lord who made you that he temper your heat now so that I may bear it when you burn me gently." When his prayer was ended, he made the sign of the cross over the fire and then remained fearless. The doctor took the glowing and hot iron in his hands; all the brothers, overcome by human weakness, fled; and the saint offered himself joyfully and eagerly to the iron.

Be on the lookout for examples of everyday miracles in the news or the stories of your acquaintances.

Prayer

The LORD is my light and my salvation;
   whom shall I fear?
The LORD is the stronghold of my life;
   of whom shall I be afraid?

—Psalm 27:1

Saturday of the First Week of Advent
GOD PROVIDES ALL WE NEED

Isaiah 30:19–21, 23–26; Psalm 147:1–2, 3–4, 5–6; Matthew 9:35—10:1, 6–8

Jesus sends his disciples out to do as he had been doing: preach the Kingdom of Heaven, heal the sick, raise the dead, cleanse lepers, drive out demons. But he was careful to remind them that they did this because they themselves had been healed and graced by God: "You received without payment; give without payment." (Matthew 10:8)

This is the ideal that the early brothers of Francis strived to live each and every day. We know that we can't always meet this ideal, but that doesn't mean it's not worth trying!

Followers of most holy poverty, because they had nothing, loved nothing, they feared in no way to lose anything. They were content with one tunic, patched at times within and without; in it was seen no refinement, but rather abjectness and cheapness, so that they might seem to be completely crucified to the world. Girt with a cord, they wore poor trousers, and they had the pious intention of remaining like this, and they wished to have nothing more. They were, therefore, everywhere secure, kept in no suspense by fear; distracted by no care, they awaited the next day without solicitude, nor were they in anxiety about the night's lodging, though in their journeyings they were often placed in great danger. For, when they frequently lacked the necessary lodging amid the coldest weather, an oven sheltered them, or at least they lay hid for the night humbly in grottos or caves. During the day, those who knew how labored with their hands, staying in the houses of lepers, or in other decent places, serving all humbly and devotedly. They did not wish to exercise any position from which scandal might arise, but always doing what is holy and just, honest and useful, they led all with whom they came into contact to follow their example of humility and patience.

Prayer

Praise the LORD!
How good it is to sing praises to our God;
    for he is gracious, and a song of praise is fitting.

…

He heals the brokenhearted,
   and binds up their wounds.
He determines the number of the stars;
   he gives to all of them their names.

                    —Psalm 147:1, 3–4

Second Sunday of Advent
THE ROUGH EDGE OF PROPHECY
Year A: Isaiah 11:1–10; Psalm 72:1–2, 7–8, 12–13, 17;
Romans 15:4–9; Matthew 2:1–12
Year B: Isaiah 40:1–5, 9–11; Psalm 85:9–10, 11–12, 13–14;
2 Peter 3:8–14; Mark 1:1–8
Year C: Baruch 5:1–9; Psalm 126:1–2, 2–3, 4–5, 6;
Philippians 1:4–6, 8–11; Luke 3:1–6

Prophets don't come into our lives every day, and they don't always make the sort of impression that John the Baptist and the biblical prophets must have made. But if we begin to understand how they experienced God, we might begin to see that even we ourselves have moments of prophetic insight. Prophets are gifted with an intense personal awareness of God's love for his people. Their call both inspires and compels them to preach this word to those who will listen—and to those who close their ears.

St. Francis's sharper edges have been somewhat softened by time and the popular imagination. But he would have understood John the Baptist. Francis accepted somewhat reluctantly the pope's command to the Lesser Brothers to preach the Word of God as they wandered the street. Once he accepted that call, he didn't hesitate to call people to repentance. But he always tempered his words with the mercy and love of God.

> We must bring forth therefore fruits befitting repentance (Luke 3:8) and love our neighbors as ourselves. Anyone who will not or cannot love his neighbor as himself should at least do him good and not do him any harm. Those who have been entrusted with the power of judging others should pass judgment mercifully just as they themselves hope to obtain mercy from God. For judgment is without mercy to him who has not shown mercy (James 2:13). We must be charitable, too, and humble, and give alms…. We lose everything which we leave behind us in this world; we can bring with us only the right to a reward for our charity and the alms we have given.

Prayer
All the ends of the earth have seen
the victory of our God.

Make a joyful noise to the LORD, all the earth;
   break forth into joyous song and sing praises.
                           —Psalm 98:3–4

Monday of the Second Week of Advent
WATER THE DESERT AND SEE WHAT HAPPENS
Isaiah 35:1–10; Psalm 85:9–10, 11–12, 13–14; Luke 5:17–26

Isaiah tells us that the desert will bloom and the parched land will rejoice. People who live in dry, hot climates see this happen again and again. But we've all seen a dry plant perk up when it gets some water. This isn't limited to the plant world. Have you also seen someone's face light up when you've done some small act of kindness for them? Try it today.

Once when the blessed Francis wanted to go to a certain hermitage that he might devote himself more freely to contemplation there, he obtained an ass from a certain poor man to ride on, because he was not a little weak. Since it was summer, the peasant, following the man of God up the mountain, became fatigued from the difficulty and the length of the trip; and before they had reached the place, he collapsed exhausted by a burning thirst. He called after the saint and begged him to have pity on him; he said he would die unless he would be refreshed by some drink. The holy man of God,

who always had compassion on those who were suffering, got down without delay from the ass and kneeling upon the ground, he stretched his hands toward heaven; and he did not let up in his prayers until he felt he had been heard. "Hurry," he said to the peasant, "and you will find living water over there, which Christ has just now mercifully brought from the rock for you to drink."....
Why should we wonder that a man who is full of the Holy Spirit should show forth in himself the wonderful deeds of all the just?

Prayer

Steadfast love and faithfulness will meet;
   righteousness and peace will kiss each other.
Faithfulness will spring up from the ground,
   and righteousness will look down from the sky.
—Psalm 85:10–12

Tuesday of the Second Week of Advent
LOOK FOR WHAT YOU'VE LOST

Isaiah 40:1–11; Psalm 96:1–2, 3, 10, 11–12, 13;
Matthew 18:12–14

Christmas specials tug at our heartstrings with stories of long-separated loved ones being reunited. God tells the prophet Isaiah: "Give comfort to my people." And Jesus tells of a shepherd leaving his flock and going in search of a stray sheep, lost and vulnerable to wolves. Francis held his brothers to high standards, but, like Jesus in whose footsteps he followed, he was always ready to forgive. He made this forgiveness part of his instructions to those who would lead the order after him.

There should be no friar in the whole world who has fallen into sin, no matter how far he has fallen, who will ever fail to find your forgiveness for the asking, if he will only look into your eyes. And if he does not ask forgiveness, you should ask him if he wants it. And should he appear before you again a thousand times, you should love him more than you love me, so that you may draw him to God;

you should always have pity on such friars. Tell the guardians, too, that this is your policy.

Prayer

The LORD is merciful and gracious,
 slow to anger and abounding in steadfast love.
He will not always accuse,
 nor will he keep his anger forever.
He does not deal with us according to our sins,
 nor repay us according to our iniquities.

—Psalm 103:8, 10

Wednesday of the Second Week of Advent
IS GOD ON YOUR "TO-DO" LIST?
Isaiah 40:25–31; Psalm 103:1–2, 3–4, 8, 10;
Matthew 11:28–30

Those who hope in the the Lord "will run and not grow weary." We might have trouble believing these words when we're running in a hundred different directions trying to get everything done. It's hard not to get caught up in the frenetic activity of the season. We want this kind of boundless energy. We can find it by keeping God as our central priority and reminding ourselves that life will go on and people will still love us, even if our errands go unfinished.

The blessed father was accustomed not to pass over any visitation of the Spirit with negligence. When indeed such was offered, he followed it, and as long as the Lord would permit, he would enjoy the sweetness thus offered him. When, therefore, while he was pressed by some business or was intent upon a journey, he felt little by little certain touches of grace, he would taste the sweetest manna…. For also along the way, with his companions going on ahead, he would stand still, and turning the new inspiration to fruitfulness, he would not receive the grace in vain.

Cross something off today's list and write in God instead.

Prayer

Bless the LORD, O my soul,
  and all that is within me,
  bless his holy name.
Bless the LORD, O my soul,
  and do not forget all his benefits.

—Psalm 103:1–2

Thursday of the Second Week of Advent
LOVE AS GOD LOVES

Isaiah 41:13–20; Psalm 145:1, 9, 10–11, 12–13;
Matthew 11:11–15

The biblical prophets have an unrelenting message: God will always be present to those who are in need, to those whose needs have gone unmet by the people around them. Contemplating such love and mercy might give us a warm, cozy feeling, yet we are also challenged to extend this same care to others.

God calls on all creation to meet the needs of his people. In return, we are called to care for all of creation. For Francis, this seemed to be deeply embedded in his nature.

In every work of the artist he praised the Artist; whatever he found in the things made he referred to the Maker. He rejoiced in all the works of the hands of the Lord and saw behind things pleasant to behold their life-giving reason and cause. In beautiful things he saw Beauty itself; all things were to him good. "He who made us is the best," they cried out to him....

He embraced all things with a rapture of unheard of devotion, speaking to them of the Lord and admonishing them to praise him. He spared lights, lamps, and candles, not wishing to extinguish their brightness with his hand, for he regarded them as a symbol of Eternal Light. He walked reverently upon stones, because of him who was called the Rock.... He forbade the brothers to cut down the whole tree when they cut wood, so that it might have hope of sprouting again....

He removed from the road little worms, lest they be crushed under foot; and he ordered that honey and the best wines be set out for the bees, lest they perish from want in the cold of winter.

Prayer

All your works shall give thanks to you, O LORD,
    and all your faithful shall bless you.

                      —Psalm 145:10

Friday of the Second Week of Advent
NAME THE SCROOGE WITHIN YOU
Isaiah 48:17–19; Psalm 1:1–2, 3, 4, 6; Matthew 11:16–19

In today's Gospel, Jesus tells the crowds that there seems to be no way to please them. He compares them to children sitting in the marketplace, saying. "We played the flute for you, and you did not dance, we wailed, and you did not mourn."

Like Ebenezer Scrooge, sometimes we can't enter into the spirit of the season. If you feel this way, don't blame the season itself or even other people's activities. Look within your heart to see what shadow may be keeping you from a wholehearted response.

Few things pained St. Francis as much as seeing his brothers criticize the people to whom they ministered and among whom they worked.

And this is my advice, my counsel, and my earnest plea to my friars in our Lord Jesus Christ that, when they travel about the world, they should not be quarrelsome or take part in disputes with words (see 2 Timothy 2:14) or criticize others; but they should be gentle, peaceful, and unassuming, courteous and humble, speaking respectfully to everyone, as is expected of them.

Prayer

Happy are those
who do not follow the advice of the wicked,
or take the path that sinners tread,
or sit in the seat of scoffers;
but their delight is in the law of the Lord,
and on his law they meditate day and night.
—Psalm 1:1–2

Saturday of the Second Week of Advent
LISTEN TO GOD'S CALL IN THE VOICES
AROUND YOU
Sirach 48:1–4, 9–11; Psalm 80:2–3, 15–16, 18–19;
Matthew 17:9a, 10–13

People on fire with zeal for justice can make us uncomfortable. We'd just as soon close our eyes to the Elijahs in our midst. But if we don't recognize Elijah, chances are we'll miss the Messiah as well. Christmas celebrates the birth of a baby in difficult circumstances a long way from home. Remember this as you invite Christ into your life today through acts of charity and justice. The challenging aspects of the Gospel may not make your life easier, but in the long run your life will be better for your openness.

Francis was such a humble, gentle man that we forget that he could be as fierce and fiery as Elijah in defense of the Gospel.

We should all realize that no matter where or how a man dies, if he is in the state of mortal sin and does not repent, when he could have done so and did not, the devil tears his soul from his body with such anguish and distress that only a person who has experienced it can appreciate it. All the talent and ability, all the learning and wisdom which he thought his own, are taken away from him, while his relatives and friends bear off his property and share it among themselves. Then they say, "A curse on his soul; he could have made more to leave to us and he did not." And the worms feast on his body. So he loses both body and soul in this short life and goes to hell, where he will be tormented without end.

Prayer

Restore us, O God;
   let your face shine, that we may be saved.

—Psalm 80:3

Third Sunday of Advent
REJOICE! THE LORD IS NEAR
Year A: Isaiah 35:1–6a, 10; Psalm 146:6–7, 8–9, 9–10;
James 5:7–10; Matthew 11:2–11
Year B: Isaiah 61:1–2a, 10–11; Luke 1:46–48, 49–50,
53–54; 1 Thessalonians 5:16–24; John 1:6–8, 19–28
Year C: Zephaniah 3:14–18a; Psalm 12:2–3, 4, 5–6;
Philippians 4:4–7; Luke 3:10–18

Advent is a time of waiting. We think of it as a time
of preparation for Christmas, and it is that. But while
we prepare, we must also be prepared to wait. Even in
our daily lives during this month of December, we find
ourselves waiting for mail deliveries, for cooking and
baking to come off the stove or out of the oven, for
Christmas trees and guests to arrive.

In his writings, St. Francis consistently counseled
both patience and joy. On this Third Sunday of Advent,
Gaudete ("Rejoice") Sunday, we might reflect on how
these two things work together.

We can never tell how patient or humble a person is when everything is going well with him. But
when those who should cooperate with him do

the exact opposite, then we can tell. A man has as much patience and humility as he has then, and no more.

Let the brothers beware lest they show themselves outwardly gloomy and sad hypocrites; but let them show themselves joyful in the Lord, cheerful and suitably gracious.

Prayer

Happy are those whose help is the God of Jacob,
   whose hope is in the LORD their God,
who made heaven and earth,
   the sea, and all that is in them;
who keeps faith forever;
   who executes justice for the oppressed;
   who gives food to the hungry.

—Psalm 146:6–7

Monday of the Third Week of Advent
LOOK THROUGH GOD'S EYES
Numbers 24:2–7, 15–17a; Psalm 25:4–5; 6–7; 8–9;
Matthew 21:23–27

The Scriptures invite us to see the world through the eyes of God. The book of Numbers tells us that God looks at the world "enraptured and with eyes unveiled." What do we see around us when we do this? Try it for one day: Look at everything and everyone around you and imagine how a creating and loving God would see what you see. Love the good; do what you can to change what needs to be changed.

> The saint said to him: "When you see a poor man, Brother, an image is placed before you of the Lord and his poor mother. So too in the sick consider the infirmities which the Lord took upon himself for us." Indeed, there was always a bundle of myrrh with Francis; he always looked on the face of his Christ, always touched the man of sorrows who was acquainted with infirmity.

Prayer

Make me to know your ways, O Lord;
    teach me your paths.
Lead me in your truth, and teach me,
    for you are the God of my salvation;
    for you I wait all day long.

—Psalm 25:4–5

Tuesday of the Third Week of Advent
IT'S OK TO SAY NO

Zephaniah 3:1–2, 9–13; Psalm 34:2–3, 6–7, 17–18, 19, 23;
Matthew 21:28–32

Sometimes being able to say no frees us to see things from a new perspective. Many of the things we do at this time of year can seem like burdens. Give yourself permission to not do joyless tasks this year. You may end up doing them anyway because you discover that they have a real value after all. But you also may find a sense of freedom in realizing that you don't have to do everything after all.

St. Francis maintained that the safest remedy against the thousand snares and wiles of the enemy is spiritual joy. For he would say: "Then the devil rejoices most when he can snatch away spiritual joy from a servant of God. He carries dust so that he can throw it into even the tiniest chinks of conscience and soil the candor of mind and purity of life. But when spiritual joy fills hearts," he said, "the serpent throws off his deadly poison in vain. The devils cannot harm the servant of Christ when they see he is filled with holy joy. When, however, the soul is wretched, desolate, and filled with sorrow, it is easily overwhelmed by its sorrow or else it turns to vain enjoyments."

Prayer

I will bless the LORD at all times;
  his praise shall continually be in my mouth.
My soul makes its boast in the LORD;
  let the humble hear and be glad.

—Psalm 34:2–3

Wednesday of the Third Week of Advent
ASSURE OTHERS OF GOD'S HEALING PRESENCE
Isaiah 45:6–8, 18, 21–25; Psalm 85:9–10, 11–12, 13–14;
Luke 7:18–23

John the Baptist, imprisoned for his efforts at preaching conversion and the Kingdom of God, felt disillusioned and may even have begun to doubt whether Jesus was the Messiah at all. Jesus assured him that the signs of compassion and healing going on around them were indeed proof that the Kingdom was at hand. Offer encouragement to all those you meet today.

Indeed, once when there was a bloody battle between the citizens of Perugia and those of Assisi, Francis was made captive with several others and endured the squalors of a prison. His fellow captives were consumed with sorrow, bemoaning miserably their imprisonment; Francis rejoiced in the Lord, laughed at his chains and despised them. His grieving companions resented his happiness and considered him insane and mad....

There was at that time among his fellow prisoners a certain proud and completely unbearable knight whom the rest were determined to shun, but Francis's patience was not disturbed. He put up with the unbearable knight and brought the others to peace with him. Capable of every grace, a chosen vessel of virtues, he poured out his gifts on all sides.

Prayer

Faithfulness will spring up from the ground,
    and righteousness will look down from the sky.
The LORD will give what is good,
    and our land will yield its increase.

—Psalm 85:11–12

Thursday of the Third Week of Advent
BE RECONCILED AND BE AT PEACE
Isaiah 54:1–10; Psalm 30:2, 4, 5–6, 11–12, 13;
Luke 7:24–30

The Lord of mercy says, "My steadfast love shall not depart from you." If you know this kind of love in your own life, you know that it frees you to reach out to others with the same kind of unconditional love. When we are reconciled with God, we feel expansive toward the world and each other. And when we are reconciled with ourselves and one another, we find God. If you haven't already done so this Advent season, find an opportunity to celebrate the sacrament of reconciliation.

We think of the saints as models of perfect virtue, but they would be the first to admit their failings. As the old saying goes, Christians aren't perfect, just forgiven.

That he might show himself in every way contemptible and give an example to the rest of true confession, Francis was not ashamed, when he had failed in something, to confess his failing in his preaching before all the people. Indeed, if it happened that he had had an evil thought about anyone, or if he had on occasion spoken an angry word, he would immediately confess his sins with all humility to the one about whom he had had the evil thought and beg his pardon. His conscience, which was a witness to his complete innocence, guarding itself with all solicitude, would not let him rest until it had gently healed the wound in his heart. Certainly he wanted to make progress in every kind of good deed, but he did not want to be looked up to on that account, but he fled admiration in every way, lest he ever become vain. But woe to us, who have lost you, worthy father, model of every good deed and of humility. By a just judgment, in truth, we have lost him whom we did not care to know when we had him.

Prayer

All praise be yours, my Lord,
through those who grant pardon
For love of you;
through those who endure sickness and trial.
Happy those who endure in peace,
By you, Most High, they will be crowned.

—"Canticle of the Creatures"

Friday of the Third Week of Advent
BUILD PEACE AND UNITY
Isaiah 56:1–3, 6–8; Psalm 67:2–3, 5, 7–8; John 5:33–36

"My house shall be called a house of prayer for all peoples." Almost without fail, it seems, this season is marred by a dispute somewhere over a religious display on government property, whether it's a Christmas crèche or a Hanukkah menorah. We don't all pray in the same way or believe the same creed. Let Isaiah's vision of a world where all people pray to a God of love and compassion inspire you to respect those who do not share your beliefs. And make sure that your own prayer and worship radiate the kind of joy and sincerity that will draw others to want to share in your celebration.

People even today marvel at Francis's journey during the Fifth Crusade and his audience with Sultan Malik al-Kamil. Here we have his first biographer's account of the meeting:

> But though he was treated shamefully by many who were quite hostile and hateful toward him, he was nevertheless received very honorably by the sultan. The sultan honored him as much as he was

able, and having given him many gifts, he tried to bend Francis's mind toward the riches of the world. But when he saw that Francis most vigorously despised all these things as so much dung, he was filled with the greatest admiration, and he looked upon him as a man different from all others. He was deeply moved by his words and he listened to him very willingly.

Prayer

May God be gracious to us and bless us
    and make his face to shine upon us,
that your way may be known upon earth,
    your saving power among all nations.
Let the peoples praise you, O God;
    let all the peoples praise you.

—Psalm 67:1–3

Fourth Sunday of Advent
TRUST GOD AND SAY YES

Year A: Isaiah 7:10–14; Psalm 24:1–2, 3–4, 5–6; Romans
1:1–7; Matthew 1:18–24

Year B: 2 Samuel 7:1–5, 8b–12, 14a, 16; Psalm 89:2–3, 4–5,
27, 29; Romans 16:25–27; Luke 1:26–38

Year C: Micah 5:1–4a; Psalm 80:2–3, 15–16, 18–19;
Hebrews 10:5–10; Luke 1:39–45

When the Spirit breaks into human life we are
confronted with an insistent challenge. We are called to
choose life or death. Joseph follows the Spirit, chooses
life and receives the assurance of Emmanuel. We, too,
are called to let the word of God break through the
confusion in our lives. If we accept its illumination in
spite of our fear, our uncertainty, our human weakness,
we will know God is with us. This is the way the birth
of Jesus comes about.

Out of the silence of Advent comes the promise of
the incarnation. The word breaks into our lives with the
startling and dazzling revelation that through Jesus of
Nazareth, God loved us in the visible, tangible ways the
angels could never understand.

For St. Francis, the incarnation was the turning point of human history. Once Christ took on human flesh in Jesus of Nazareth, the salvation fulfilled in the resurrection was set in motion. Francis's commitment to poverty and humility had its roots in the incarnation. His love for Mary, the Mother of God, was based on her role in giving birth to the incarnate Lord.

Francis says of the events in today's Gospel: "Our Lord Jesus Christ is the glorious Word of the Father, so holy and exalted, whose coming the Father made known by St. Gabriel the Archangel to the glorious and blessed Virgin Mary, in whose womb he took on our weak human nature. He was rich beyond measure and yet he and his holy Mother chose poverty."

When we grasp how Francis understood the mystery of the incarnation, we begin to make sense of all he said and did in living and proclaiming the Gospel. In this Christmas season, we can take Francis's reverence for the Nativity as our model and guide in all the ways we celebrate God's love.

Prayer

Hail, holy Lady,
Most holy Queen,

Mary, Mother of God,
Ever Virgin;
Chosen by the most holy Father in heaven,
Consecrated by him,
With his most holy beloved Son
And the Holy Spirit, the Comforter.
On you descended and in you still remains
All the fulness of grace And every good.

Note: Eight days before Christmas, the Lectionary
provides a separate cycle of readings for
December 17–24.

The O Antiphons

The last days of Advent are set aside to reflect on the meaning of the first Christmas, on the salvation Christ's birth brings to his time, to our time, to all time. The Gospel antiphons for these days at Mass and at Evening Prayer have come to be known as the "O antiphons." We may know them best as the verses of the ancient Advent hymn "O Come, O Come Emmanuel. They name the Christ who comes into our world to set us free. Francis would have known and prayed these antiphons.

December 17
"O WISDOM"
Genesis 49:2, 8–10; Psalm 72:3–4, 7–8, 17; Matthew
1:1–17

As Christmas approaches and the lists of things to do overwhelm us, tension and anxiety increase. We may also be afraid that our own hopes and dreams for Christmas this year will be disappointed. The wisdom of Advent helps us find our way through the expectations of the season. We find our way to a deeper source of peace and joy that we can hold on to when everything around us seems to argue against it.

Where there is Love and Wisdom, there is neither
Fear nor Ignorance.
Where there is Patience and Humility, there is neither Anger nor Annoyance.
Where there is Poverty and Joy, there is neither
Cupidity nor Avarice.
Where there is Peace and Contemplation, there is
neither Care nor Restlessness.
Where there is the Fear of God to guard the dwelling, there no enemy can enter.

Where there is Mercy and Prudence, there is neither Excess nor Harshness.

Prayer

May the mountains yield prosperity for the people,
and the hills, in righteousness.
May he defend the cause of the poor of the people,
give deliverance to the needy,
and crush the oppressor.

—Psalm 72:3–4

December 18
"O LORD"
Jeremiah 23:5–8; Psalm 72:1, 12–13, 18–19;
Matthew 1:18–24

"O sacred Lord of ancient Israel, who showed yourself to Moses in the burning bush, who gave him the holy law on Sinai mountain: Come, stretch out your mighty hand to set us free." We sometimes do what we do during the holidays only out of a sense of duty. Like Moses, we need to experience the burning bush of God's loving and liberating presence among us. We need to let the true spirit of Christmas restore the fire of love to actions that have grown cold and empty.

Francis wanted such men to be ministers of the word of God who give themselves to the study of spiritual things and are not hindered by other duties. For these, he used to say, have been chosen by a certain great king to deliver to the people the edicts that proceed from his mouth. But he said: "The preacher must first draw from secret prayers what he will later pour out in holy sermons; he must first grow hot within before he speaks words that are in themselves cold." He said that this is an office to be revered and that those who administer it should be reverenced by all. "These," he said, "are the life of the body; they are the attackers of the devils; they are the light of the world."

Prayer

Blessed be the LORD, the God of Israel,
    who alone does wondrous things.
Blessed be his glorious name for ever;
    may his glory fill the whole earth.

—Psalm 72:18–19

December 19
"O FLOWER OF JESSE'S STEM"
Judges 13:2–7, 24–25; Psalm 71:3–4, 5–6, 16–17;
Luke 1:5–25

Bethlehem's Jesse was the father of David, who became Israel's greatest king. Born in David's royal line, Jesus flowered as the fulfillment of the hopes of his people. We, too, stand out as flowers of love and grace in the lives of our loved ones. Think of someone who brings God's love into your life. Find a special way to say thank you. A poinsettia or Christmas cactus can serve as a reminder of the flower of Jesse.

How great a gladness do you think the beauty of the flowers brought to his mind when he saw the shape of their beauty and perceived the odor of their sweetness? He used to turn the eye of consideration immediately to the beauty of that flower that comes from the root of Jesse and gives light in the days of spring and by its fragrance has raised innumerable thousands from the dead. When he found an abundance of flowers, he preached to them and invited them to praise the Lord as though they were endowed with reason. In the same way he exhorted with the sincerest purity cornfields and vineyards, stones and forests and all the beautiful things of the fields, fountains of water and the green things of the gardens, earth and fire, air and wind, to love God and serve him willingly.

Prayer

For you, O LORD, are my hope,
  my trust, O LORD, from my youth.
Upon you I have leaned from my birth;
  it was you who took me from my mother's womb.
My praise is continually of you.

—Psalm 71:5–6

December 20
"O KEY OF DAVID"
Isaiah 7:10–14; Psalm 24:1–2, 3–4, 5–6; Luke 1:26–38

"O Key of David, O Royal power of Israel, controlling at your will the gate of heaven: Come break down the prison walls of death for those who dwell in darkness and the shadow of death."

At this festive time of year, when all our attention seems focused on gathering with loved ones, those who are grieving face a most difficult challenge. They may feel locked out of the brightness around them. Be the key that releases those who are grieving, while still respecting their own journey. Reach out to those who have lost special people in their lives. Be creative. Spending a quiet evening with a friend may be more consoling than an invitation to share in festivities with a heavy heart.

During the days when Francis was staying at Rieti to have his eyes cared for, he called one of his companions who had been a lute player in the world, saying: "Brother, the children of this world do not understand the hidden things of God. For musical

instruments that were once destined for the praises
of God, lust has changed into a means of pleasure
for the ears. Therefore, Brother, I would like for
you to borrow a lute secretly and bring it here so
that with it you may give some wholesome comfort to brother body that is so full of pains." The
brother replied: "I am not a little ashamed to do
so, Father, because I am afraid men may suspect
that I am being tempted to frivolity." The saint
said: "Let us then forget about it, Brother. It is
good to give up many things so that the opinion of
others may not be harmed." The next night, when
the saint was watching and meditating about God,
suddenly there came the sound of a lute of wonderful harmony and very sweet melody. No one
was seen, but the volume of the sound marked the
going and coming of the lute player as he moved
back and forth. Finally, with his spirit fixed on
God, the holy father enjoyed so much the sweetness in that melodious song that he thought he had
been transported to another world. When he got
up in the morning he called the aforementioned
brother and telling him everything just as it had

happened, he added: "The Lord who consoles the afflicted has never left me without consolation. For behold, I who could not hear the lutes of men have heard a far sweeter lute."

Prayer

Who shall ascend the hill of the LORD?
    And who shall stand in his holy place?
Those who have clean hands and pure hearts,
    who do not lift up their souls to what is false,
    and do not swear deceitfully.

—Psalm 24:3–4

December 21
"O Radiant Dawn"
Song of Songs 2:8–14 or Zephaniah 3:14–18; Psalm
33:2–3, 11–12, 20–21; Luke 1:39–35

People in all times and cultures have celebrated the shortest day of the year, clinging to the belief that the sun will not continue to diminish. In a sense, we may share in this primal sense of hope and fear any time we experience a long stretch of gray cloud cover. Christ, like the rising sun dispelling gloom and dreariness, cheers us immeasurably. If today is cloudy, hold on to the hope that the sun is still there. If today is sunny, do something outside to celebrate the radiant Son of God.

Although this blessed man had been educated in none of the branches of learning, still, grasping the wisdom that is of God from above and enlightened by the rays of eternal light, he had a deep understanding of the Scriptures. For his genius, free from all stain, penetrated the hidden things of mysteries, and where the knowledge of the masters is something external, the affection of one who loves enters within the thing itself. At times he would read the sacred books and what he put into his mind once he wrote indelibly in his heart. His memory substituted for books, for he did not hear a thing once in vain, for his love meditated on it with constant devotion. This he would say was a fruitful way of learning and reading, not by wandering about through thousands of treatises. Him he considered a true philosopher who put nothing before his desire for eternal life. But he often said that that man would easily move from knowledge of himself to a knowledge of God who would set himself to study the Scriptures humbly, not presumptuously. He often explained doubtful questions word for word, and though he was unskilled in words, he set forth the sense and meaning admirably.

Prayer

Rejoice in the LORD, O you righteous.
Praise befits the upright.
Praise the LORD with the lyre;
make melody to him with the harp of ten strings.
Sing to him a new song;
play skillfully on the strings, with loud shouts.

—Psalm 33:1

December 22

"O KING OF THE NATIONS"
1 Samuel 1:24–28; 1 Samuel 2:1, 4–5, 6–7, 8abcd;
Luke 1:46–56

We celebrate Christ as the King of all the nations, the prince of peace. Conflict in the world seems like an affront to our faith, particularly at this time of year. Conflict in our families can be heightened because of stress. Rather than lose heart, we need to look for possibilities for reconciliation. Christ joins heaven and earth, bridging the distance that separates people from one another.

Francis's understanding of his relationship to the Lord was shaped by the culture of chivalry, feudal lords and the knights who did their bidding. One of the formative visions in his conversion called him to serve the Lord God instead of an inferior human lord.

Accordingly, while he was sleeping one night, someone addressed him a second time in a vision and questioned him solicitously as to whether he intended to go. When he had told his purpose to him who was asking and said that he was going to

Apulia to fight, he was asked earnestly who could do better for him, the servant or the Lord. And Francis said: "The Lord." The other answered: "Why then are you seeking the servant in place of the Lord?" And Francis said: "Lord, what do you want me to do?" And the Lord said to him: "Go back to the place of your birth for through me your vision will have a spiritual fulfillment."

Prayer

The LORD makes poor and makes rich;
  he brings low, he also exalts.
He raises up the poor from the dust;
  he lifts the needy from the ash heap,
to make them sit with princes
  and inherit a seat of honor.

—1 Samuel 2:7, 8

December 23
"O Emmanuel"
Malachi 3:1–4, 23–24: Psalm 25:4–5, 8–9, 10, 14;
Luke 1:57–66

Emmanuel is perhaps the most familiar name we give to God during Advent. It means "God with us." For a people who longed for the Messiah through the centuries, Emmanuel named the fulfillment of all their dreams. We believe that God is with us today and every day. Take time today to think about your deepest desire for this Christmas season. How is God's presence part of the fulfillment of that desire?

Today's Gospel tells of the birth of John the Baptist. Because Francis often characterized himself as the herald of the Great King, it's not surprising that his biographers would see in his mother's desire to name him Giovanni (John) a sign of his identification from birth with the forerunner of the Messiah.

Francis, the servant and friend of the Most High, to whom divine providence gave this name so that by means of this singular and unusual name the knowledge of his ministry might become known to the whole world, was called John by his mother, when, being born again of water and the Holy Spirit, he was made a child of grace from a child of wrath…. For while her neighbors were wondering at the nobility of soul and the modesty of Francis, she would say, as though prompted by divine guidance: "What do you think this my son will turn out to be? Know that he will be a son of God by the grace of his merits."

This indeed was the opinion of not a few whom the youthful Francis pleased by reason of his good inclinations…. He considered the feast of John the Baptist to be more illustrious than the feasts of all the other saints, for the dignity of his name left a mark of mystic virtue upon him.

Prayer

And you, child, will be called the prophet of the
   Most High;
   for you will go before the Lord to prepare his ways,
to give knowledge of salvation to his people
   by the forgiveness of their sins.

—Luke 1:76–79

December 24

<small>PAUSE BEFORE THE WONDER OF THE INCARNATION</small>
Isaiah 9:1–6; Psalm 96:1–2, 2–3, 11–12, 13; Titus 2:11–14;
Luke 2:1–14 (Mass at Midnight)

We take nativity scenes and Christmas crèches for granted today, but in fact St. Francis was the first to imagine that first Christmas in such humble detail.

The humility of the incarnation and the charity of the passion occupied his memory particularly, to the extent that he wanted to think of hardly anything else. What he did on the birthday of our Lord Jesus Christ near the little town called Greccio in the third year before his glorious death should especially be noted and recalled with reverent memory. In that place there was a certain man by the name of John, of good reputation and an even better life, whom blessed Francis loved with a special love, for in the place where he lived he held a noble and honorable position in as much as he had trampled upon the nobility of his birth and pursued nobility of soul. Blessed Francis sent for this man, as he often did, about fifteen days before the birth of the Lord, and he said to him: "If you want us to celebrate the present feast of our Lord at Greccio, go with haste and diligently prepare what I tell you. For I wish to do something that will recall to memory the little Child who was born in Bethlehem and set before our bodily eyes in some way the inconveniences of his infant needs, how he lay in a manger, how, with an ox and an ass standing by, he lay upon the hay where he had been placed." When the good and faithful man heard these things, he ran with haste and prepared in that place all the things the saint had told him.

But the day of joy drew near, the time of great rejoicing came. The brothers were called from their various places. Men and women of that neighborhood prepared with glad hearts, according to their means, candles and torches to light up that night that has lighted up all the days and years with its gleaming star. At length the saint of God came, and finding all things prepared, he saw it and was glad. The manger was prepared, the hay had been brought, the ox and ass were led in. There simplicity was honored, poverty was exalted, humility was commended, and Greccio was made, as it were, a new Bethlehem. The night was lighted up like the day, and it delighted men and beasts. The people came and were filled with new joy over the new mystery. The woods rang with the voices of the crowd and the rocks made answer to their jubilation. The brothers sang, paying their debt of praise to the Lord, and the whole night resounded with their rejoicing. The saint of God stood before the manger, uttering sighs, overcome with love, and filled with a wonderful happiness. The solemnities of the Mass were celebrated over the manger and the priest experienced a new consolation.

The saint of God was clothed with the vestments of the deacon, for he was a deacon, and he sang the holy Gospel in a sonorous voice. And his voice was a strong voice, a sweet voice, a clear voice, a sonorous voice, inviting all to the highest rewards. Then he preached to the people standing about, and he spoke charming words concerning the nativity of the poor King and the little town of Bethlehem. Frequently too, when he wished to call Christ Jesus, he would call him simply the

Child of Bethlehem, aglow with overflowing love for him; and speaking the word Bethlehem, his voice was more like the bleating of a sheep. His mouth was filled more with sweet affection than with words. Besides, when he spoke the name Child of Bethlehem or Jesus, his tongue licked his lips, as it were, relishing and savoring with pleased palate the sweetness of the words. The gifts of the Almighty were multiplied there, and a wonderful vision was seen by a certain virtuous man. For he saw a little child lying in the manger lifeless, and he saw the holy man of God go up to it and rouse the child as from a deep sleep. This vision was not unfitting, for the Child Jesus had been forgotten in the hearts of many; but, by the working of his grace, he was brought to life again through his servant St. Francis and stamped upon their fervent memory. At length the solemn night celebration was brought to a close, and each one returned to his home with holy joy.

The hay that had been placed in the manger was kept, so that the Lord might save the beasts of burden and other animals through it as he multiplied his holy mercy. And in truth it so happened that many animals throughout the surrounding region that had various illnesses were freed from their illnesses after eating of this hay. Indeed, even women laboring for a long time in a difficult birth, were delivered safely when some of this hay was placed upon them; and a large number of persons of both sexes of that place, suffering from various illnesses, obtained the health they sought. Later, the place on which the manger had stood was made sacred by a temple of the Lord, and an altar was built in honor of the most blessed father Francis over the manger and a church was built, so that where once the animals had eaten the hay, there in the future men would eat unto health of soul and body the flesh of the lamb without blemish and without spot, our Lord Jesus Christ, who in highest and ineffable love gave himself to us, who lives and reigns with the Father and the Holy Spirit, God, eternally glorious, forever and ever. Amen. Alleluia, Alleluia.

Prayer

    O come, let us adore him,
    O come, let us adore him,
    O come, let us adore him,
    Christ the Lord.

December 25
ALL CREATION REJOICES
Isaiah 52:7–10; Psalm 98:1, 2–3, 3–4, 5–6; Hebrews
1:1–16; John 1:1–18

The celebration of Christmas begins on Christmas Eve and extends through the feast of the Epiphany. This gives us almost two weeks to celebrate the incarnation. For Francis, the wonder of the Son of God becoming a vulnerable human child shaped his approach to all of creation.

On this day Francis wanted the poor and the hungry to be filled by the rich, and more than the usual amount of grain and hay given to the oxen and asses. "If I could speak to the emperor," he said, "I would ask that a general law be made that all who can should scatter corn and grain along the roads so that the birds might have an abundance of food on the day of such great solemnity, especially our sisters the larks." He would recall, not without tears, what great want surrounded the poor Virgin on that day. Once when he was sitting at dinner, a certain brother talked about the poverty of the

Blessed Virgin and recalled the want of Christ, her
Son. Francis immediately arose from the table and,
with great sighs and many tears, ate the rest of the
meal on the bare ground.

Prayer

In the beginning was the Word,
and the Word was with God,
and the Word was God.
The light shines in the darkness,
and the darkness did not overcome it.

—John 1:1, 5

December 26
COMPASSION FOR THE POOR
Acts 6:8–10; 7:54–59; Psalm 31:3–4, 6, 8ab, 16bc, 17;
Matthew 10:17–22

On the day after Christmas, we celebrate the feast of the first Christian martyr. Because St. Stephen was a deacon in the early Church, charged with the care of widows and orphans, many cultures celebrate his feast day by making a special effort to help the poor. This would please St. Francis.

The man of God feared a multitude in his solicitude for poverty, for a multitude has the appearance of wealth, if indeed it is not in fact wealthy. Hence he used to say: "Oh, if it were possible, my wish would be that the world would see the Friars Minor but rarely and be filled with wonder at the smallness of their number!" Therefore, bound to the Lady Poverty by an indissoluble bond, he looked for her dowry not in the present life, but in the future. He used to chant with more fervent affections and greater rejoicing those psalms that speak of poverty, for instance: "The patience of the poor shall not perish forever," and "Let the poor see and rejoice."

Prayer

Into your hand I commit my spirit;
  you have redeemed me, O LORD, faithful God.

—Psalm 31:5

December 27
THE WORD MADE FLESH
1 John 1:1–4; Psalm 97:1–2, 5–6, 11–12; John 20:1a, 2–8

Today we celebrate the feast of St. John the Evangelist. His Gospel tells us again and again that God is love. And it is in his Prologue, even more than in the infancy narratives of Matthew and Luke that we hear the great mystery of the incarnation: "And the Word became flesh and lived among us" (John 1:14).

Since the strength of Francis's love made him a brother to all other creatures, it is not surprising that the charity of Christ made him more than a brother to those who are stamped with the image of their Creator. For he used to say that nothing is more important than the salvation of souls, and he often offered as proof the fact that the Only-begotten of God deigned to hang on the cross for souls. This accounts for his struggles at prayer, his tirelessness at preaching, his excess in giving examples. He did not consider himself a friend of Christ unless he loved the souls that Christ loved. And this was the main reason why he reverenced doctors so much, namely, because, as Christ's helpers, they exercised one office with him. He loved his brothers beyond measure with an affection that rose from his innermost being, because they were of the same household of faith and united by participation in an eternal inheritance according to the promise.

Prayer

And the Word became flesh and lived among us,
and we have seen his glory,
the glory as of a father's only son,
full of grace and truth.

—John 1:14

December 28

HOLY INNOCENTS

1 John 1:5—2:2; Psalm 124:2-3, 4-5, 7cd-8;
Matthew 2:13-18

Today's feast commemorates the children Herod had slaughtered in his crazed search for the newborn king he feared would supplant him. How Francis would have wept over this story, loving as he did the infant Jesus. Throughout his writings and his words to his brothers, he railed against the sort of ambition that would have driven a ruler like Herod.

Humility is the guardian and the ornament of all virtues. If the spiritual building does not rest upon it, it will fall to ruin, though it seems to be growing. This virtue filled Francis in a more copious abundance, so that nothing should be wanting to a man adorned with so many gifts. In his own opinion, he was nothing but a sinner, despite the fact that he was the ornament and splendor of all sanctity. He tried to build himself up upon this virtue, so that he would lay the foundation he had learned from Christ. Forgetting the things he had gained, he set before his eyes only his failings in the conviction that he lacked more than he had gained. There was no covetousness in him except the desire to become better, and not content with what he had, he sought to add new virtues.... All lofty speaking was absent from his mouth, all pomp from his gestures, all ostentation from his actions.

Prayer

We have escaped like a bird
    from the snare of the fowlers;
the snare is broken,
    and we have escaped.

Our help is in the name of the LORD,
    who made heaven and earth.

—Psalm 124:7–8

December 29
GOD'S LOVE IN A TINY CHILD
1 John 2:3–11; Psalm 96:1–2a, 2b–3, 5b–6; Luke 2:22–35

Today we hear the story of the presentation of Jesus in the Temple. We've all seen the way the eyes of nursing home residents light up when a child comes to visit. We can picture Anna and Simeon, both elderly and devoted to the Lord's promise, cooing over the infant Jesus but still recognizing the significance of his place in the history of salvation.

The birthday of the Child Jesus Francis observed with inexpressible eagerness over all other feasts, saying that it was the feast of feasts, on which God, having become a tiny infant, clung to human breasts. Pictures of those infant members he kissed with thoughts filled with yearning, and his compassion for the Child flooded his heart and made him stammer words of sweetness after the manner of infants. His name was like honey and the honeycomb in Francis's mouth.

Prayer

> Master, now you are dismissing your servant in peace,
>> according to your word;
> for my eyes have seen your salvation,
>> which you have prepared in the presence of all
>> peoples,
> a light for revelation to the Gentiles
>> and for glory to your people Israel.

—Luke 2:29–32

December 30
FEAST OF THE HOLY FAMILY
Sirach 3:2–6, 12–14; Psalm 128:1–2, 3, 4–5; Colossians
3:12–21; Luke 2:41–52

We need to celebrate today's feast not as some seemingly unattainable goal for mere humans, but as a sign of the obstacles that we can overcome if we truly place ourselves in the arms of a loving God who is Father and Mother to us all, and in whose sight we are all part of a holy and sacred family.

One of the stories nearly everyone knows about St. Francis is that he publicly and dramatically rejected his father, Pietro, in order to follow his call from God. In this, as in so many other things, he is following Christ, who said that anyone who did not leave mother and father, sisters and brothers, to follow him was not worthy to be called a disciple.

We struggle with this part of the Gospel in different ways throughout our lives. As young people, we might embrace a sense of freedom from our families. As parents, however, we might be reluctant to let our children go.

In his *Testament,* written a year or two before his death, Francis tells the story of his call. And in his words, we see the promise of Christ once again coming to fulfillment. Francis has left mother, father, sisters, and brothers. And then he tells us that at the very beginning of his new life, "the Lord gave me brothers."

Even as we celebrate the Feast of the Holy Family and continue our Christmas festivities with our own families, we know that as Christians, we have been given mothers and fathers, sisters and brothers, in a communion that extends far beyond the ties of biology. This is the promise of the Good News.

Prayer

Happy is everyone who fears the Lord,
    who walks in his ways.
You shall eat the fruit of the labor of your hands;
    you shall be happy, and it shall go well with you.

                              —Psalm 128:1–2

December 31
SING TO THE LORD
1 John 2:18–21; Psalm 96:1–2, 11–12, 13; John 1:1–18

On the liturgical calendar, today bears the pedestrian title "Seventh Day in the Octave of Christmas." The readings for today's Mass once again recount the great mystery of the Incarnation. Our everyday world is gearing up for New Year's Eve parties. Francis was no stranger to parties. In his youth, they occupied most of his time and energy. After his conversion, he still retained a love for music, now channeling those high spirits into praise of God.

> Sometimes Francis would act in the following way. When the sweetest melody of spirit would bubble up in him, he would give exterior expression to it in French, and the breath of the divine whisper which his ear perceived in secret would burst forth in French in a song of joy. At times, as we saw with our own eyes, he would pick up a stick from the ground and putting it over his left arm, would draw across it, as across a violin, a little bow bent by means of a string; and going through the

motions of playing, he would sing in French about his Lord. This whole ecstasy of joy would often end in tears and his song of gladness would be dissolved in compassion for the passion of Christ. Then this saint would bring forth continual sighs, and amid deep groanings, he would be raised up to heaven, forgetful of the lower things he held in his hand.

Prayer

O sing to the Lord a new song;
    sing to the Lord, all the earth.
Sing to the Lord, bless his name;
    tell of his salvation from day to day.

—Psalm 96:1–2

January 1

MARY, MOTHER OF GOD

Numbers 6:22–27; Galatians 4:4–7; Psalm 67:2–3, 5, 6, 8;
Luke 2:16–21

Today's feast reminds us that God's gracious and loving touch always comes to us in very human ways. The mystery of the incarnation that we celebrate in this Christmas season revolves around God taking on our human flesh and dwelling in our midst so that we might become one with him in that love. Marian feasts, besides pointing to Christ, also tell us something about our own lives and the life of the Church. St. Luke tells us that after the shepherds left, Mary "treasured all these things in her heart."

We've all had experiences that have been so overwhelming that we have no words for them. We hold them close to protect them from the ordinary push and pull of everyday life. We turn them over and reflect on them until we find a way to share what can be shared. Like Mary, we need to learn to treasure all these things as gifts from a gracious God.

Like many of the saints, St. Francis had a special devotion to Mary, the Mother of God. His favorite church in Assisi, the Portiuncula or "Little Portion" was dedicated to St. Mary of the Angels.

Then he went to another place, which is called the Portiuncula, where there stood a church of the Blessed Virgin Mother of God that had been built in ancient times, but was now deserted and cared for by no one. When the holy man of God saw how it was thus in ruins, he was moved to pity, because he burned with devotion toward the mother of all good; and he began to live there in great zeal. It was the third year of his conversion when he began to repair this church.

Prayer

Hail, his Palace.
Hail, his Tabernacle.
Hail, his Robe.
Hail, his Handmaid.
Hail, his Mother.
And Hail, all holy Virtues,
Who, by the grace

And inspiration of the Holy Spirit,
Are poured into the hearts of the faithful
So that, faithless no longer,
They may be made faithful servants of God through
    you.

January 2
KEEPING IT REAL
1 John 2:22–28; Psalm 98:1, 2–3ab, 3cd–4; John 1:19–28

The days of Christmas are winding down. We return to work, to school, to the realities of our everyday lives. Most of us don't have the luxury of celebrating the twelve days of Christmas. Perhaps most people never did. It may have been reserved for the aristocracy, the nobles, the people who didn't have to work for a living. Francis was familiar with the great gap between the wealthy and the poor in Assisi. His own family was in the newly emerging merchant class, but he left even that degree of comfort behind and went to live with the poor and the outcast. Much of the Church hierarchy, however, still lived in luxury.

> Once when St. Francis visited Pope Gregory of happy memory, when the latter was still placed in a lower station, and the hour of dinner was at hand, he went out for alms, and returning, placed some of the scraps of black bread on the bishop's table. When the bishop saw this, he was somewhat ashamed, above all because of the newly invited

guests. The father, however, with a joyous countenance distributed the alms he had received to the knights and the chaplains gathered about the table; all of them accepted the alms with wonderful devotion, and some of them ate them, others kept them out of reverence. When the dinner was finished, the bishop arose and taking the man of God to an inner room, he raised his arms and embraced him. "My Brother," he said, "why did you bring shame on me in the house that is yours and your brothers by going out for alms?" The saint said to him: "Rather I have shown you honor, for I have honored a greater lord. For the Lord is well pleased with poverty, and above all with that poverty that is voluntary. For I have a royal dignity and a special nobility, namely, to follow the Lord who, being rich, became poor for us." And he added: "I get more delight from a poor table that is furnished with small alms than from great tables on which dainty foods are placed almost without number." Then, greatly edified, the bishop said to the saint: "Son, do what seems good in your eyes, for the Lord is with you."

Prayer

You are love,
You are wisdom.
You are humility,
You are endurance.
You are rest,
You are peace.
You are joy and gladness.
You are justice and moderation.

January 3
THE HOLY NAME OF JESUS
1 John 2:29—3:6; Psalm 98:1, 3cd–4, 5–6; John 1:29–34

Today we celebrate the memorial of the Holy Name of Jesus. We don't give this feast as much attention as it once had in the Church calendar, but it might be good to look at it through the eyes of St. Francis. Most of us find ourselves using the Lord's name in something other than prayer from time to time. For Francis, the name of the Lord was so sacred that any writing bore something of the sacred about it.

> For he was filled with love that surpasses all human understanding when he pronounced your holy name, O holy Lord; and carried away with joy and purest gladness, he seemed like a new man, one from another world. Therefore, whenever he would find anything written, whether about God or about man, along the way, or in a house, or on the floor, he would pick it up with the greatest reverence and put it in a sacred or decent place, so that the name of the Lord would not remain there or anything else pertaining to it. One day when he

was asked by a certain brother why he so diligently picked up writings even of pagans or writings in which there was no mention of the name of the Lord, he replied: "Son, because the letters are there out of which the most glorious name of the Lord God could be put together. Whatever is good there does not pertain to the pagans, nor to any other men, but to God alone, to whom belongs every good." And what is no less to be admired, when he had caused some letters of greeting or admonition to be written, he would not allow even a single letter or syllable to be deleted, even though they had often been placed there superfluously or in error.

Prayer

Blessed be God.
Blessed be His Holy Name.
Blessed be Jesus Christ, true God and true man.
Blessed be the name of Jesus.
Blessed be His Most Sacred Heart.
Blessed be His Most Precious Blood.
Blessed be Jesus in the Most Holy Sacrament
    of the Altar.
Blessed be the Holy Spirit, the Paraclete.

Blessed be the great Mother of God, Mary most holy.
Blessed be her holy and Immaculate Conception.
Blessed be her glorious Assumption.
Blessed be the name of Mary, Virgin and Mother.
Blessed be Saint Joseph, her most chaste spouse.
Blessed be God in His angels and in His Saints.

January 4
THE GREATEST GIFT
1 John 3:7–10; Psalm 98:1, 7–8, 9; John 1:35–42

As we approach the Feast of Epiphany, we might take time to reflect on the many gifts we exchange during this celebration of Christmas. Don't forget the intangible gifts of love, friendship, time spent with family and friends. Our material possessions are only worth as much as they bring us closer to God and to one another.

Once the mother of two of the brothers came to the saint confidently asking an alms. The holy father had pity on her and said to his vicar, Brother Peter of Catania: "Can we give some alms to our mother?" Francis was accustomed to call the mother of any brother his mother and the mother of all the brothers. Brother Peter answered him: "There is nothing left in the house that could be given her." And he added: "We have one New Testament from which we read the lessons at Matins since we do not have a breviary." Blessed Francis said to him: "Give the New Testament to our mother that she might sell it to take care of her needs, since we are admonished by it to help the poor. I believe indeed that the gift of it will be more pleasing to God than our reading from it." The book, therefore, was given to the woman, and thus the first Testament that was in the order was given away through this holy kindness.

Prayer

You are all our riches,
And you suffice for us.
You are beauty.
You are gentleness.
You are our protector,
You are our guardian and defender.
You are courage.
You are our haven and our hope.
You are our faith,
Our great consolation.
You are our eternal life, Great and wonderful
Lord, God almighty,
Merciful Savior.

January 5
BECOMING A PRAYER
1 John 3:11–21; Psalm 100:1b–2, 3, 4, 5; John 1:43–51

Take a deep breath! The twelve days of Christmas conclude tomorrow. Our celebration of Advent and Christmas has brought us closer to God, given us a new awareness of the humanity of Christ, and given us new ways to celebrate the incarnation. On this day before the Feast of Epiphany, we take a moment to pray with St. Francis, learning from his example how to be present to the Lord in our prayer.

When he prayed in the woods and in solitary places, he would fill the woods with sighs, water the places with his tears, strike his breast with his hand, and discovering there a kind of secret hiding place, he would often speak with his Lord with words. There he would give answer to his judge; there he would offer his petitions to his father; there he would talk to his friend; there he would rejoice with the bridegroom. Indeed, that he might make his whole being a holocaust in many ways, he would set before his eyes in many ways him who is simple to the greatest degree. Often, without moving his lips, he would meditate within himself and drawing external things within himself, he would lift his spirit to higher things. All his attention and affection he directed with his whole being to the one thing which he was asking of the Lord, not so much praying as becoming himself a prayer.

Prayer

You are holy, Lord, the only God, and your deeds
  are wonderful.
You are strong.
You are great.
You are the Most High,
You are almighty.
You, holy Father, are King of heaven and earth.
You are Three and One,
Lord God, all good.
You are Good, all Good, supreme Good,
Lord God, living and true.

January 6
Feast of the Epiphany
Isaiah 60:1–6; Psalm 72:1–2, 7–8, 10–11, 12–13; Ephesians
3:2–3a, 5–6; Matthew 2:1–12

Today we celebrate the Epiphany. This is one of those
feasts that has been linked in popular culture to the
visit of the Three Kings to the child Jesus. We see men
in luxurious robes and camels decked with gifts for the
infant king, notably gold, frankincense and myrrh. The
popular carol "We Three Kings" echoes in our heads
and exotic images of the East swirl around us. It's easy
to distance ourselves from the story of the Epiphany, to
see it as a movie set or a grand opera. But our tradition
and our Scriptures remind us that we, too, have a part
to play in the great story of salvation. Our roles might
not be center stage, but we each have unique gifts to
offer the world. We are called, first and foremost, to
bring those gifts to the newborn King, the Messiah, the
Christ Child, the Lord of all who was born in a humble
stable in Bethlehem.

If we take away the costumes and the drama and the
decorations of this feast, we see the story at its finest:

the gifts we offer to God are transformed into something far greater than anything we could ever imagine: the gift of eternal life in communion with the divine.

Franciscan Father Murray Bodo writes: "It is a Franciscan teaching that Christ would have come and lived among us whether or not we had sinned. The Incarnation was in the divine plan from all eternity. It was divine love that caused the Incarnation to happen. But because we had become captive to sin, Christ willed to redeem us through his cross and blood and death. This is a great mystery that moves Francis to give thanks to God" (*The Simple Way: Meditations on the Words of Saint Francis*).

Prayer

We thank you that through your Son you created us,
and through the holy love you had for us
you brought about his birth as true God and
   true man
by the glorious, ever-virgin, most blessed, holy Mary,
and that you willed to redeem us captives
through his cross and blood and death.

About the Author

Diane M. Houdek is the digital media editor for Franciscan Media, as well as author and editor of *Bringing Home the Word* and a senior editor of *Liberty+Vine*. She has written extensively for Franciscan Media, and is a past editor of *Scripture From Scratch* and *Weekday Homily Helps*.